PRINCEWILL LAGANG

The Resilient Entrepreneur: Thriving in Uncertain Times

Contents

1

The Resilient Entrepreneur: Thriving in Uncertain Times

In the world of entrepreneurship, the path to success is rarely a straight line. It's a journey marked by highs and lows, successes and failures, and above all, uncertainty. The entrepreneur's life is an ever-evolving adventure, where adaptability and resilience become the keys to not just survival, but thriving in the face of adversity. This chapter, titled "The Resilient Entrepreneur: Thriving in Uncertain Times," sets the stage for a journey into the mindset, skills, and strategies necessary for navigating the turbulent waters of entrepreneurship and emerging stronger on the other side.

The Entrepreneur's Dilemma

Imagine this: You've just embarked on your entrepreneurial journey. You have a brilliant idea, a business plan, and the drive to make it a reality. You can visualize the success, the freedom, and the impact your venture will have on the world. But as you take your first steps, you quickly realize that the path ahead is far from smooth.

The road to entrepreneurship is fraught with challenges, from financial instability to fierce competition, unexpected market shifts, and personal sacrifices. In recent years, the global business landscape has become even more unpredictable, with disruptions like economic downturns, pandemics, and rapid technological advancements constantly reshaping the entrepreneurial terrain. Uncertainty, it seems, is the new normal.

Yet, in the face of such adversity, resilient entrepreneurs thrive. They don't just survive; they find opportunity in chaos, strength in setbacks, and growth in uncertainty. This chapter explores the qualities that set resilient entrepreneurs apart and offers a roadmap for developing these essential attributes.

The Essence of Resilience

Resilience is the ability to bounce back from setbacks, adapt to change, and keep moving forward. Resilient entrepreneurs possess a unique blend of characteristics that help them not only weather the storms but harness their power for growth. These characteristics include:

1. Adaptability
   Resilient entrepreneurs are quick to pivot, adjust their strategies, and embrace change. They view challenges as opportunities for growth and learning, rather than insurmountable obstacles.

2. Grit
   Grit is the relentless determination to achieve long-term goals. Resilient entrepreneurs exhibit unwavering persistence, even when faced with adversity. They understand that success often requires taking many small steps, and they are committed to enduring the journey.

3. Emotional Intelligence
   Emotional intelligence allows entrepreneurs to navigate the complex world

of relationships, manage stress, and make decisions that benefit not only their businesses but also the well-being of those around them. It's a vital tool for effective leadership in turbulent times.

4. Resourcefulness

Resilient entrepreneurs are masters of resourcefulness. They can do more with less, find creative solutions to problems, and tap into a diverse network of contacts to support their endeavors.

5. Self-Care

Entrepreneurship can be all-consuming, but resilient individuals recognize the importance of self-care. They know that maintaining physical and mental well-being is essential for long-term success.

The Roadmap to Resilience

Becoming a resilient entrepreneur is a journey in itself. It requires self-awareness, continuous learning, and a commitment to personal growth. This chapter will explore each of the aforementioned characteristics in-depth, offering practical strategies and real-life examples from successful entrepreneurs who have thrived in the face of uncertainty.

As you delve into the pages ahead, consider the challenges you've faced in your entrepreneurial journey. Reflect on how resilience, adaptability, grit, emotional intelligence, resourcefulness, and self-care can be integrated into your life and business. In the end, you'll come to understand that resilience isn't just a quality; it's a way of life for the modern entrepreneur, a source of strength that can transform adversity into opportunity and uncertainty into growth.

2

Building Resilience Through Adaptability

In Chapter 1, we explored the essence of resilience and the characteristics that set resilient entrepreneurs apart. Now, let's dive deeper into the first critical trait: adaptability. Adaptability is the entrepreneur's superpower, the ability to pivot, evolve, and thrive in an ever-changing landscape. In this chapter, we will examine the importance of adaptability and provide practical strategies for building this essential skill.

The Power of Adaptability

Imagine you're sailing a ship in uncharted waters. The wind shifts, the currents change, and you encounter unexpected obstacles. In this situation, adaptability is your compass. It helps you navigate through uncertainty, adjust your course, and continue towards your destination, even when the path is unclear.

Entrepreneurs who embrace adaptability view change as an opportunity rather than a threat. They recognize that the business world is dynamic and that rigid, inflexible strategies can lead to failure. Instead, they remain open to new information, willing to revise their plans, and ready to innovate.

The Entrepreneur's Dilemma: Change or Perish

In today's fast-paced business environment, the saying "change or perish" holds more truth than ever. Technological advancements, market fluctuations, and unforeseen disruptions can quickly render a business model obsolete. The ability to adapt becomes a matter of survival.

Strategies for Building Adaptability

1. Cultivate a Growth Mindset: Embrace challenges as opportunities to learn and grow. A growth mindset fosters a willingness to adapt because it sees setbacks as a chance to improve.

2. Stay Informed: Continuously gather data and insights about your industry and market. An adaptable entrepreneur is well-informed and can make decisions based on the latest information.

3. Foster a Culture of Adaptability: Encourage adaptability within your team or organization. Create an environment where change is expected and valued, and where employees are empowered to contribute ideas for improvement.

4. Set Short-Term Goals: While long-term vision is essential, it's equally important to set achievable short-term goals. This allows you to make regular adjustments as you progress toward your larger objectives.

5. Embrace Technology: Leverage technology to streamline operations and respond to changes more rapidly. Automation and data analysis tools can help you adapt in real-time.

6. Seek Feedback: Listen to your customers, employees, and mentors. Constructive feedback can reveal areas where adaptation is necessary.

7. Experiment and Innovate: Allocate resources for experimentation and

innovation. Test new strategies and products, and be willing to pivot if you discover a better way forward.

Real-Life Examples

Consider the case of Blockbuster, a once-dominant video rental chain. Despite its massive success, Blockbuster failed to adapt to the rise of digital streaming and was eventually rendered obsolete. In contrast, Netflix, a DVD-by-mail service at the time, recognized the changing landscape and pivoted to streaming, becoming a global powerhouse.

Similarly, companies like Amazon and Google continually adapt and innovate, expanding their product and service offerings. Their ability to pivot quickly in response to market trends has contributed to their ongoing success.

The Journey to Adaptability

Becoming more adaptable is a lifelong journey. It requires a commitment to learning, a willingness to embrace change, and the courage to step out of your comfort zone. In the chapters ahead, we'll explore other traits that complement adaptability, such as grit, emotional intelligence, and resourcefulness, as we build a comprehensive roadmap to becoming a resilient entrepreneur. Adaptability is just the first step on this transformative journey, helping you navigate the uncertain waters of entrepreneurship with confidence and purpose.

3

Navigating Uncertainty with Grit

In Chapter 2, we explored the importance of adaptability in building resilience as an entrepreneur. Now, let's delve into another essential trait: grit. Grit is the unwavering determination and perseverance to overcome obstacles, a quality that empowers entrepreneurs to stay the course and achieve long-term goals, no matter the challenges they face.

The True Grit of Entrepreneurs

As you embark on your entrepreneurial journey, you'll quickly realize that setbacks and obstacles are part and parcel of the experience. Whether it's financial struggles, market volatility, or personal doubts, you'll face numerous moments when the easy choice would be to give up. However, it's during these trying times that grit becomes your greatest ally.

The Entrepreneur's Dilemma: Challenges on the Path

Entrepreneurs often find themselves in situations where the road ahead seems insurmountable. It's easy to become disheartened and question your choices when faced with rejection, failure, or seemingly endless difficulties. This is where grit sets the successful entrepreneur apart from the rest.

The Components of Grit

Grit is composed of two main components, as identified by psychologist Angela Duckworth:

1. Passion: The intense desire and commitment to achieving long-term goals. This passion fuels your drive to persist through adversity.

2. Perseverance: The ability to stick with your goals, even when the journey becomes difficult or tiresome. Perseverance keeps you moving forward in the face of setbacks.

Strategies for Building Grit

1. Define Your Passion: To develop grit, you must be deeply passionate about your entrepreneurial endeavors. Reflect on why you started your venture and the impact you want to make on the world. Passion will be your anchor during challenging times.

2. Set Clear Goals: Define your long-term goals and break them down into smaller, manageable milestones. This makes the path to success more achievable and less daunting.

3. Embrace Failure as a Learning Opportunity: Instead of seeing failure as the end, view it as a stepping stone toward success. Every setback is a chance to learn and grow.

4. Practice Self-Discipline: Build routines and habits that keep you on track, even when motivation wanes. Self-discipline is essential for maintaining momentum.

5. Seek Support and Mentorship: Connect with a network of peers and mentors who can provide guidance, encouragement, and a fresh perspective during tough times.

6. Celebrate Small Wins: Recognize and celebrate the small achievements along the way. These victories will help maintain your motivation and drive.

7. Maintain a Growth Mindset: A growth mindset embraces challenges and views effort as a path to mastery. This mindset keeps you focused on long-term growth rather than short-term obstacles.

Real-Life Examples

One of the most famous examples of entrepreneurial grit is Elon Musk. Despite numerous setbacks, criticism, and financial challenges, Musk remained committed to his vision of space exploration and electric vehicles. His companies, SpaceX and Tesla, have revolutionized their respective industries and achieved incredible success.

Another example is J.K. Rowling, the author of the Harry Potter series. She faced rejection from multiple publishers before finally finding success. Her unwavering commitment to her writing and her ability to persevere in the face of adversity eventually led her to become one of the best-selling authors in history.

The Journey to Grit

Developing grit as an entrepreneur is a journey that requires continuous effort and resilience. It's not about avoiding challenges but facing them head-on with determination. Grit is the foundation upon which your adaptability, emotional intelligence, and other resilient qualities will rest. As we progress through this exploration of entrepreneurship, remember that grit will be your constant companion, helping you overcome the obstacles that inevitably arise on your path to success.

4

Emotional Intelligence: The Heart of Resilient Leadership

I n our journey to explore the qualities that make resilient entrepreneurs, we have discussed adaptability and grit. Now, we turn our attention to a fundamental trait that underlies successful leadership in the face of uncertainty: emotional intelligence.

The Power of Emotional Intelligence

Emotional intelligence, often abbreviated as EQ, is the ability to recognize, understand, manage, and effectively use emotions in ourselves and others. In the entrepreneurial world, EQ is a game-changer. It enables leaders to navigate complex human interactions, make well-informed decisions, and inspire teams in times of upheaval.

The Entrepreneur's Dilemma: Emotions in Business

Entrepreneurship is a rollercoaster of emotions. Successes, failures, and the daily challenges of running a business can trigger a wide range of feelings. In times of crisis or uncertainty, emotions can run particularly high, affecting not only your own well-being but also the dynamics within your team and the relationships with customers, partners, and investors.

The Components of Emotional Intelligence

Emotional intelligence consists of several key components:

1. Self-Awareness: Recognizing your own emotions and understanding their impact on your thoughts and behaviors.

2. Self-Regulation: Managing your emotions and controlling impulsive reactions, especially during high-stress situations.

3. Empathy: Understanding and relating to the emotions of others, which is crucial for effective communication and collaboration.

4. Social Skills: Building positive relationships, inspiring and influencing others, and managing conflicts constructively.

Strategies for Developing Emotional Intelligence

1. Practice Self-Awareness: Regularly check in with yourself to identify your emotions and their sources. Journaling, meditation, and self-reflection can be helpful tools.

2. Manage Stress: Develop healthy coping mechanisms for stress, such as exercise, mindfulness, or hobbies that bring you joy.

3. Seek Feedback: Ask for honest feedback from peers, mentors, and team members to gain insights into how your emotions affect those around you.

4. Empathize with Others: Actively listen and put yourself in others' shoes to

better understand their perspectives and emotions.

5. Improve Communication: Learn to express your thoughts and feelings clearly and empathetically. Encourage open and honest communication within your team.

6. Develop Conflict Resolution Skills: Embrace conflict as an opportunity for growth and practice constructive conflict resolution techniques.

7. Lead by Example: Demonstrate emotional intelligence in your leadership style, showing your team how to navigate emotions effectively.

Real-Life Examples

Steve Jobs, the co-founder of Apple Inc., was known for his visionary leadership. However, he was also notorious for his intense emotions and high standards. Later in his career, Jobs developed greater emotional intelligence. He learned to balance his passion for perfection with more effective ways of communicating with his team and collaborators.

Richard Branson, the founder of the Virgin Group, is another entrepreneur who exemplifies emotional intelligence. His ability to connect with people, build relationships, and inspire those around him has played a significant role in the success of his diverse business ventures.

The Journey to Emotional Intelligence

Building emotional intelligence is an ongoing process that can significantly enhance your resilience as an entrepreneur. Emotional intelligence is the key to fostering a positive and productive work environment, managing stress, and effectively leading through times of uncertainty. As you continue your entrepreneurial journey, remember that your EQ can be as influential as your IQ, shaping not only your success but also the success of your team and your ventures.

5

Resourcefulness: Thriving with Limited Resources

In our exploration of resilient entrepreneurship, we've examined adaptability, grit, and emotional intelligence as essential traits. Now, in Chapter 5, we turn our attention to another critical quality: resourcefulness. Resourcefulness is the ability to find creative and effective solutions to challenges, often in the face of limited resources. It empowers entrepreneurs to do more with less and turn constraints into opportunities.

The Art of Resourcefulness

Entrepreneurship often begins with limited capital, personnel, and other resources. Resourcefulness is your entrepreneurial superpower, enabling you to stretch your limited resources, solve problems, and make progress in the absence of abundant assets.

The Entrepreneur's Dilemma: Doing More with Less

Starting and growing a business on a shoestring budget is a common reality for many entrepreneurs. Limited resources can be a challenge, but they can also be a catalyst for innovation and creative problem-solving.

The Elements of Resourcefulness

Resourcefulness involves several key elements:

1. Creativity: The ability to think outside the box and generate unconventional ideas and solutions.

2. Adaptability: Being open to change and willing to pivot when necessary to address resource constraints.

3. Networking: Building a diverse network of connections and collaborators who can provide support, advice, and resources.

4. Efficiency: Streamlining processes and operations to maximize the use of available resources.

5. Frugality: A conscious effort to use resources judiciously and avoid unnecessary expenses.

Strategies for Developing Resourcefulness

1. Cultivate a Growth Mindset: Embrace challenges as opportunities for creative problem-solving and resourcefulness.

2. Diversify Your Network: Build relationships with individuals and organizations that can provide support, whether it's financial, mentorship, or access to resources.

3. Regularly Review and Optimize Processes: Continuously assess your business operations and look for ways to improve efficiency.

4. Learn from Others: Study successful entrepreneurs who have overcome resource constraints and adapt their strategies to your own situation.

5. Prioritize and Focus: Concentrate your efforts on activities and projects that have the most significant impact and maximize the use of your available resources.

6. Experiment and Test: Be willing to try new approaches and experiment with different strategies to determine what works best.

7. Seek Feedback: Ask for input from mentors, advisors, or team members to gain insights into areas where resourcefulness can be enhanced.

Real-Life Examples

Airbnb is a prime example of resourcefulness. The company's founders, Brian Chesky and Joe Gebbia, found themselves struggling to pay rent in San Francisco. They noticed a local shortage of affordable accommodations during conferences and decided to rent out their living room to attendees, providing a simple solution to a common problem. This concept evolved into the global Airbnb platform.

Another example is Dropbox, co-founded by Drew Houston. When Houston needed a file-sharing solution for his personal use, he couldn't find a satisfactory one. He leveraged his technical skills and limited resources to create Dropbox, a solution that has since become a widely used cloud storage and file-sharing service.

The Journey to Resourcefulness

Resourcefulness is a skill that can be developed and refined over time. It not only helps entrepreneurs overcome resource constraints but also fosters innovation and adaptability. As you continue your entrepreneurial journey, remember that resourcefulness is the key to turning limitations into opportunities, helping you achieve your goals and thrive in the face of uncertainty.

6

Self-Care: Nurturing the Entrepreneurial Spirit

I n our exploration of resilient entrepreneurship, we've discussed several crucial qualities, including adaptability, grit, emotional intelligence, and resourcefulness. Now, in Chapter 6, we delve into a vital yet often overlooked aspect of entrepreneurial success: self-care. Self-care is the practice of prioritizing your physical, mental, and emotional well-being to maintain resilience and sustain long-term entrepreneurial growth.

The Importance of Self-Care

Entrepreneurship is often associated with relentless hustle and round-the-clock dedication. While hard work is essential, neglecting self-care can lead to burnout, diminished productivity, and reduced creativity. Resilient entrepreneurs understand that taking care of themselves is not a luxury but a necessity.

The Entrepreneur's Dilemma: Balancing Passion and Well-Being

Entrepreneurs are passionate about their endeavors, but this passion can sometimes lead to neglecting their own needs. Long hours, high stress, and constant pressure can take a toll on physical and mental health.

The Components of Self-Care

Self-care involves several key components:

1. Physical Well-Being: Prioritizing exercise, nutrition, and sufficient sleep to maintain good health and energy levels.

2. Mental Health: Recognizing the importance of stress management, mindfulness, and relaxation techniques to support mental well-being.

3. Emotional Balance: Developing emotional resilience and strategies for coping with the highs and lows of entrepreneurship.

4. Work-Life Balance: Striking a balance between work and personal life to prevent burnout and maintain relationships.

5. Learning and Growth: Continuously seeking personal and professional development to foster creativity and adaptability.

Strategies for Prioritizing Self-Care

1. Set Boundaries: Establish clear boundaries between work and personal life. Avoid overworking and make time for relaxation and hobbies.

2. Practice Mindfulness: Incorporate mindfulness techniques, such as meditation and deep breathing, into your daily routine to manage stress and improve focus.

3. Stay Active and Eat Well: Regular exercise and a balanced diet are essential

for physical health and mental clarity.

4. Get Sufficient Sleep: Prioritize quality sleep to rejuvenate your body and mind. Sleep is essential for cognitive function and emotional well-being.

5. Seek Professional Help: Don't hesitate to seek help from mental health professionals or coaches when needed. Mental health should be a priority, and seeking assistance is a sign of strength, not weakness.

6. Schedule Time for Personal Growth: Dedicate time for learning and personal development. This can help you stay adaptable and creative in your entrepreneurial endeavors.

7. Connect with a Support System: Maintain close relationships with friends, family, and mentors who can provide emotional support and guidance.

Real-Life Examples

A well-known example of an entrepreneur who emphasizes self-care is Arianna Huffington, co-founder of The Huffington Post. After experiencing burnout herself, she became an advocate for sleep and self-care, authoring books like "The Sleep Revolution" to promote well-being as an essential part of success.

Another example is Mark Cuban, the billionaire entrepreneur, and owner of the Dallas Mavericks. He emphasizes the importance of a healthy lifestyle, stating that regular exercise and sufficient sleep are integral to his success as an entrepreneur.

The Journey to Self-Care

In the relentless world of entrepreneurship, self-care is often underestimated but should be a cornerstone of resilience. As you continue your entrepreneurial journey, remember that taking care of yourself is not a sign of weakness but a source of strength. Prioritizing self-care ensures that you are not only resilient but also equipped for long-term growth and success in the face of uncertainty.

7

Building a Resilient Team

In the previous chapters, we explored the qualities and strategies that can help you, as an entrepreneur, develop resilience. However, no entrepreneurial journey is a solitary one. In this chapter, we'll shift our focus to the importance of building a resilient team. A cohesive and adaptable team is a cornerstone of entrepreneurial success, and as a leader, it's your responsibility to foster an environment where your team can thrive in uncertain times.

The Role of a Resilient Team

A resilient team is one that can adapt to change, collaborate effectively, and collectively overcome challenges. Such teams are invaluable assets in the ever-evolving landscape of entrepreneurship.

The Entrepreneur's Dilemma: Leading in Uncertainty

Entrepreneurs often find themselves leading teams through uncharted territories. Whether you're dealing with market fluctuations, product pivots, or unforeseen crises, your ability to guide your team plays a crucial role in your business's success.

Nurturing a Resilient Team

Building a resilient team involves several components:

1. Effective Communication: Transparent and open communication is essential for keeping the team informed, engaged, and aligned with the company's goals.

2. Cohesiveness: Fostering a sense of belonging and trust among team members encourages collaboration and mutual support.

3. Adaptability: Encourage your team to embrace change and pivot when necessary. Resilient teams are quick to adjust to new circumstances.

4. Innovation and Creativity: Create an environment that welcomes new ideas and solutions. Empower your team to think outside the box.

5. Conflict Resolution: Equip your team with effective conflict resolution skills to handle disputes constructively.

Strategies for Building a Resilient Team

1. Lead by Example: Demonstrate resilience, adaptability, and emotional intelligence in your own leadership. Your team will look to you for guidance.

2. Prioritize Team Well-Being: Promote self-care and well-being within your team. Encourage breaks, support mental health, and provide opportunities for growth.

3. Foster Open Communication: Create a culture where team members feel comfortable sharing their ideas, concerns, and feedback.

4. Set Clear Goals: Ensure that your team understands your business's long-term vision and the steps necessary to reach it.

5. Provide Continuous Learning Opportunities: Invest in the development of your team through training, mentorship, and skill-building programs.

6. Celebrate Achievements: Acknowledge and celebrate the team's successes, both big and small. Recognition boosts morale and motivation.

7. Support Diversity and Inclusion: Encourage diversity and inclusion within your team. Diverse perspectives can lead to more creative problem-solving.

Real-Life Examples

One of the most celebrated examples of a resilient team is the one behind SpaceX, led by Elon Musk. SpaceX has accomplished numerous milestones in the aerospace industry, including reusable rocket technology and affordable space travel. The company's culture emphasizes innovation, adaptability, and learning from failures.

Another example is Pixar Animation Studios. The Pixar team, under the leadership of Steve Jobs and others, has consistently delivered groundbreaking films, thanks to their commitment to collaboration and creativity. They have built a culture of resilience and excellence in the world of animation.

The Journey to a Resilient Team

Fostering a resilient team requires strong leadership, effective communication, and a supportive environment. As you continue your entrepreneurial journey, remember that your team is an essential part of your success. By building a resilient team, you create a network of support and innovation that can help you navigate uncertainty and reach new heights in your entrepreneurial endeavors.

8

The Entrepreneur's Guide to Risk Management

In the world of entrepreneurship, risk is an ever-present companion. In this chapter, we will explore the importance of risk management for resilient entrepreneurs. Successful business leaders understand that embracing risk is often a necessary part of growth, but effective risk management is equally vital to ensure long-term success.

Understanding Risk in Entrepreneurship

Risk is inherent in entrepreneurship. It can take various forms, including financial risk, market risk, operational risk, and more. Resilient entrepreneurs recognize that risk can be both a catalyst for innovation and a potential source of setbacks.

The Entrepreneur's Dilemma: Balancing Risk and Reward

Entrepreneurs often find themselves in situations where risk is necessary to drive growth. However, unchecked risk-taking can lead to financial and reputational consequences. Striking the right balance is essential.

The Elements of Effective Risk Management

Effective risk management involves the following elements:

1. Risk Assessment: Identifying and understanding the types of risks that your business may face, both internal and external.

2. Risk Mitigation: Implementing strategies to reduce or eliminate potential risks before they materialize.

3. Risk Transfer: Shifting some of the risk to other parties, such as through insurance or partnerships.

4. Risk Acceptance: Recognizing that some level of risk is unavoidable and being prepared to handle the consequences.

5. Contingency Planning: Preparing for potential risks by creating plans and resources to manage adverse events.

Strategies for Effective Risk Management

1. Identify and Prioritize Risks: Start by identifying the potential risks your business faces and prioritizing them based on their potential impact and likelihood.

2. Implement Risk Mitigation Strategies: Develop and execute strategies to reduce risks. This may involve diversifying your product line, investing in security measures, or creating a crisis management plan.

3. Stay Informed: Regularly monitor industry trends, market conditions, and other factors that may affect your business.

4. Maintain a Financial Cushion: Keep a financial reserve to handle unexpected expenses or financial setbacks.

5. Seek Professional Advice: Consult with experts, such as legal advisors or risk management specialists, to help you identify and mitigate risks effectively.

6. Test and Adjust: Continuously test your risk management strategies and adjust them as needed. Learning from experience can help you refine your approach.

7. Crisis Management Plan: Develop a crisis management plan that outlines the steps to be taken in the event of a major risk materializing. Ensure your team is familiar with the plan and knows their roles.

Real-Life Examples

One of the most well-known examples of effective risk management is seen in Amazon's journey. Amazon, initially an online bookseller, continually diversified its product offerings to mitigate market risk. This strategy transformed it into a global e-commerce giant with a diverse range of products and services.

Warren Buffett, often considered one of the world's most successful investors, is a master of risk management. His "Margin of Safety" principle involves investing in businesses with a significant financial cushion to withstand economic downturns and unforeseen events.

The Journey to Effective Risk Management

Effective risk management is a vital aspect of resilience for entrepreneurs. While embracing calculated risks can lead to significant rewards, it's equally important to have a strategy for managing and mitigating potential pitfalls. As you continue your entrepreneurial journey, remember that risk management is not about avoiding risk entirely but about understanding, preparing for, and managing it to ensure your business's long-term success.

29

9

Building Resilience through Continuous Learning

As we near the end of our journey into the world of resilient entrepreneurship, we focus on a fundamental quality that underpins adaptability and long-term success: continuous learning. In this chapter, we'll explore how entrepreneurs can thrive in uncertain times by fostering a growth mindset and committing to lifelong learning.

The Power of Continuous Learning

Entrepreneurs who embrace continuous learning recognize that the world is constantly evolving. To stay ahead in a dynamic business environment, they must evolve too. Continuous learning is the process of acquiring new knowledge, skills, and perspectives throughout one's entrepreneurial journey.

The Entrepreneur's Dilemma: Stagnation or Growth

The business landscape is ever-changing, driven by technological advancements, shifting market trends, and unforeseen events. Entrepreneurs who fail to adapt and learn may find their ventures stagnating or becoming obsolete.

The Components of Continuous Learning

Continuous learning encompasses several key components:

1. Curiosity: A natural curiosity and a hunger for new knowledge and experiences.

2. Adaptability: A willingness to adapt and evolve based on new insights and changing circumstances.

3. Resilience: Learning from setbacks and using them as opportunities for growth.

4. Mentorship: Seeking guidance from experienced mentors who can provide valuable insights and lessons.

5. Feedback: Actively seeking feedback from customers, peers, and team members to refine strategies and approaches.

6. Self-Directed Learning: Taking the initiative to seek out new information and opportunities for growth.

Strategies for Continuous Learning

1. Set Learning Goals: Establish clear learning objectives and milestones to guide your growth.

2. Read Widely: Consume a diverse range of books, articles, and resources to broaden your knowledge.

3. Take Courses and Workshops: Enroll in courses, workshops, and webinars

that are relevant to your field.

4. Attend Conferences and Events: Participate in industry conferences and networking events to connect with experts and stay updated on trends.

5. Learn from Failure: Instead of dwelling on setbacks, analyze them for lessons and opportunities for improvement.

6. Teach and Share Knowledge: Teaching others reinforces your own learning and deepens your understanding of a subject.

7. Stay Open-Minded: Be open to new ideas and differing perspectives. Continuous learning often involves unlearning old habits and embracing new approaches.

Real-Life Examples

Elon Musk, the founder of SpaceX, Tesla, and other ventures, exemplifies the spirit of continuous learning. Musk has been involved in various industries, from electric vehicles to space exploration. His commitment to learning and adapting is evident in his ability to lead groundbreaking companies in multiple sectors.

Oprah Winfrey, an accomplished entrepreneur and media mogul, is known for her dedication to lifelong learning. She has consistently sought out mentors and continues to explore various areas, from journalism to book publishing to film and television production.

The Journey to Continuous Learning

Continuous learning is the foundation of adaptability and resilience in the entrepreneurial world. It ensures that you remain at the forefront of your field, ready to pivot and innovate when necessary. As you continue your entrepreneurial journey, remember that learning is not a destination but a lifelong process that can fuel your growth, resilience, and long-term success.

10

Fostering Resilience in Your Entrepreneurial Ecosystem

In this final chapter of our journey into resilient entrepreneurship, we will explore how you can foster resilience not only within yourself but also within your broader entrepreneurial ecosystem. Your ability to build and contribute to a resilient network of entrepreneurs, partners, and communities can be a powerful force for positive change and growth.

The Entrepreneurial Ecosystem

The entrepreneurial ecosystem consists of a network of interconnected entities, including entrepreneurs, startups, investors, mentors, and support organizations. By fostering resilience within this ecosystem, you contribute to the collective strength and adaptability of the entrepreneurial community.

The Entrepreneur's Dilemma: Interdependence and Resilience

Entrepreneurs do not exist in isolation. They are interconnected and reliant on a network of resources, guidance, and collaboration. Fostering resilience within this ecosystem benefits all its participants.

Nurturing a Resilient Ecosystem

Building a resilient entrepreneurial ecosystem involves several components:

1. Collaboration: Encouraging entrepreneurs and organizations to work together, share knowledge, and support one another.

2. Mentorship: Providing guidance and mentorship to new entrepreneurs to help them navigate challenges and setbacks.

3. Access to Resources: Ensuring that entrepreneurs have access to the resources they need, from funding to education and training.

4. Inclusivity: Promoting diversity and inclusivity within the ecosystem to harness a wide range of perspectives and experiences.

5. Community Engagement: Involving entrepreneurs and organizations in the community to create a supportive environment.

Strategies for Fostering Resilience in the Ecosystem

1. Network and Connect: Actively seek out opportunities to connect with fellow entrepreneurs, investors, and support organizations in your ecosystem.

2. Mentorship: Pay it forward by mentoring and supporting less experienced entrepreneurs. Your guidance can be invaluable in helping others overcome challenges.

3. Invest in Education: Support educational programs and initiatives that provide valuable skills and knowledge to aspiring entrepreneurs.

4. Support Inclusivity: Promote inclusivity and diversity within your network and seek out opportunities to provide resources and mentorship to underrepresented groups.

5. Advocate for Entrepreneurial Policies: Get involved in advocating for policies that support entrepreneurship and small business growth.

6. Collaborate on Projects: Partner with other entrepreneurs and organizations on collaborative projects that benefit the ecosystem as a whole.

Real-Life Examples

Y Combinator, a startup accelerator, exemplifies the power of fostering resilience within an entrepreneurial ecosystem. They provide funding and mentorship to early-stage startups, contributing to the growth of countless successful companies, including Dropbox, Airbnb, and Reddit.

The Kauffman Foundation, a non-profit organization, supports entrepreneurship through research and initiatives that help create a thriving entrepreneurial ecosystem. Their work has helped drive innovation and economic growth in various regions.

The Journey to a Resilient Entrepreneurial Ecosystem

Fostering resilience within the entrepreneurial ecosystem is a way to contribute to the collective strength of entrepreneurs, startups, and support organizations. By nurturing a supportive, collaborative, and inclusive network, you create an environment that empowers everyone to thrive and adapt in the face of uncertainty. As you continue your entrepreneurial journey, remember that your impact extends beyond your own ventures, and your efforts to build a resilient ecosystem can be a catalyst for positive change and growth.

11

Sustaining Resilience for the Long Haul

As we conclude our exploration of resilient entrepreneurship, we focus on the importance of sustaining resilience over the long term. Building resilience is an ongoing journey, and it requires consistent effort and commitment. In this final chapter, we'll discuss strategies for maintaining and reinforcing your resilience as you continue your entrepreneurial journey.

The Ongoing Journey of Resilience

Resilience is not a one-time achievement but an ongoing process. Your ability to navigate uncertainty and overcome challenges will be tested repeatedly as you pursue your entrepreneurial goals.

The Entrepreneur's Dilemma: The Test of Time

Over the course of your entrepreneurial career, you will face a multitude of trials and tribulations. Sustaining resilience becomes essential to withstand the test of time.

Strategies for Sustaining Resilience

1. Reflect and Learn: Continuously assess your experiences and learn from them. Reflect on your setbacks and successes to gain insights and refine your strategies.

2. Stay Adaptable: The business landscape is always changing. Stay adaptable and open to new ideas and strategies.

3. Reinforce Your Network: Maintain and expand your network of mentors, peers, and support organizations. They can provide valuable guidance and support.

4. Practice Self-Care: Prioritize self-care to ensure you remain physically and mentally fit for the challenges ahead.

5. Set New Goals: Regularly set new goals and milestones to stay motivated and maintain your sense of purpose.

6. Celebrate Achievements: Don't forget to acknowledge and celebrate your achievements. Recognizing your progress can boost your morale and motivation.

7. Embrace Failure: Failure is a part of entrepreneurship. Embrace it as a learning opportunity and don't be discouraged by setbacks.

8. Pass on Knowledge: As you gain experience, consider mentoring others and sharing your knowledge. Teaching can reinforce your own understanding.

Real-Life Examples

A prime example of an entrepreneur who has sustained resilience over the long term is Richard Branson, the founder of the Virgin Group. Branson has continuously adapted and diversified his business ventures, from music to airlines to space travel, over the decades.

Warren Buffett, known for his long and successful career in investing, has maintained resilience by sticking to his investment principles and embracing change as markets evolve.

The Journey to Sustaining Resilience

Sustaining resilience is a lifelong commitment for entrepreneurs. As you continue your journey, remember that it's not only about building resilience in the short term but also about maintaining it over the long haul. With ongoing reflection, adaptability, self-care, and a willingness to learn, you can remain resilient and continue to thrive in the face of uncertainty and change. Your entrepreneurial journey is a testament to your capacity for growth, innovation, and resilience.

12

The Resilient Entrepreneur's Legacy

In our final chapter, we explore the enduring impact of resilient entrepreneurship. As you look back on your journey and consider the legacy you want to leave, it's essential to reflect on the lasting influence you can have on your industry, community, and the world. Your legacy as a resilient entrepreneur goes beyond business success; it's about the mark you leave on the people and the world around you.

Defining Your Entrepreneurial Legacy

Your entrepreneurial legacy is a reflection of the principles, values, and achievements that you want to be remembered for. It encompasses the lessons you've learned, the relationships you've built, and the positive change you've inspired.

The Entrepreneur's Dilemma: Leaving a Mark

Entrepreneurs have the power to create lasting change, not only through their ventures but also by influencing others and contributing to their communities.

Strategies for Shaping Your Legacy

1. Define Your Values: Clarify the values and principles that guide your entrepreneurial journey. Your legacy should be an extension of these core beliefs.

2. Pay It Forward: Mentor and support the next generation of entrepreneurs, sharing your knowledge and experiences to help others succeed.

3. Promote Positive Change: Use your resources and influence to drive positive change in your industry or community, whether it's through social responsibility initiatives or advocacy.

4. Document Your Journey: Share your story and experiences through writing, speaking, or other forms of communication. Your journey can inspire and educate others.

5. Build Sustainable Ventures: Create businesses that prioritize sustainability and social responsibility, leaving a positive impact on the environment and society.

6. Foster Inclusivity: Champion diversity and inclusivity within your entrepreneurial ecosystem, ensuring that opportunities are accessible to a wide range of individuals.

7. Live Your Values: Your actions should align with your values. Be a role model for the principles you stand for.

Real-Life Examples

Muhammad Yunus, the founder of Grameen Bank and a pioneer of microcredit, has left a powerful entrepreneurial legacy. His work has lifted millions of people out of poverty through access to small loans, sparking a global movement in microfinance.

Anita Roddick, the founder of The Body Shop, built a business that prioritized environmental sustainability, ethical sourcing, and social responsibility. Her legacy continues to influence the cosmetics industry and inspire other entrepreneurs to embrace ethical business practices.

The Journey to Leaving a Legacy

As you conclude your journey as a resilient entrepreneur, remember that your legacy is a reflection of the positive and enduring impact you've had on the world. It's not just about your personal success, but about the difference you've made in the lives of others and the contributions you've made to your community and industry. Your legacy is a testament to the power of resilience, innovation, and entrepreneurship to create meaningful and lasting change.

In this comprehensive guide, we've explored the world of resilient entrepreneurship across twelve chapters, covering essential qualities, strategies, and principles for success in the face of uncertainty. Here's a summary of the key takeaways from each chapter:

Chapter 1: "The Resilient Entrepreneur: Thriving in Uncertain Times"
  - Resilient entrepreneurship is the ability to adapt, persist, and thrive in the face of challenges.
  - Embrace uncertainty as an opportunity for growth and innovation.

Chapter 2: "Adaptability: Navigating Change with Grace"
  - Adaptability is the skill of adjusting to changing circumstances.
  - Cultivate adaptability through a growth mindset and flexibility.

Chapter 3: "Grit: The Power of Perseverance"
  - Grit is the determination and persistence to overcome obstacles and achieve long-term goals.

- Develop grit by setting clear goals, staying focused, and maintaining passion.

Chapter 4: "Emotional Intelligence: The Heart of Resilient Leadership"
- Emotional intelligence (EQ) is crucial for effective leadership and team management.
- Components of EQ include self-awareness, self-regulation, empathy, and social skills.

Chapter 5: "Resourcefulness: Thriving with Limited Resources"
- Resourcefulness is the ability to find creative solutions to challenges with limited resources.
- Foster resourcefulness through creativity, adaptability, and efficient use of resources.

Chapter 6: "Self-Care: Nurturing the Entrepreneurial Spirit"
- Self-care is essential for maintaining physical, mental, and emotional well-being.
- Prioritize self-care through practices like mindfulness, exercise, and work-life balance.

Chapter 7: "Building a Resilient Team"
- A resilient team can adapt to change and overcome challenges together.
- Cultivate resilience within your team through effective communication, adaptability, and support.

Chapter 8: "The Entrepreneur's Guide to Risk Management"
- Risk management is crucial for mitigating potential setbacks in entrepreneurship.
- Identify, assess, and mitigate risks to balance innovation and caution effectively.

Chapter 9: "Fostering Resilience through Continuous Learning"

- Continuous learning is essential for staying adaptable and innovative in entrepreneurship.

- Cultivate a growth mindset, set learning goals, and embrace lifelong learning.

Chapter 10: "Fostering Resilience in Your Entrepreneurial Ecosystem"
- Fostering resilience in the entrepreneurial ecosystem benefits all participants.

- Collaborate, mentor, and support inclusivity to create a resilient and supportive network.

Chapter 11: "Sustaining Resilience for the Long Haul"
- Sustaining resilience is a lifelong journey that requires adaptability and self-care.

- Reflect on your experiences, stay adaptable, and continue learning to maintain resilience.

Chapter 12: "The Resilient Entrepreneur's Legacy"
- Your entrepreneurial legacy extends beyond business success to your impact on people and the world.

- Define your values, support positive change, and live your values to leave a lasting legacy.

This guide serves as a comprehensive roadmap for entrepreneurs to navigate the challenges and uncertainties of their journey, fostering resilience, and making a positive and enduring impact on their entrepreneurial ecosystem and the world.

www.ingramcontent.com/pod-product-compliance
Lightning Source LLC
LaVergne TN
LVHW021314200726
843509LV00012B/1918